Play Piano with. Adele

WISE PUBLICATIONS
PART OF THE MUSIC SALES GROUP
LONDON / NEW YORK / PARIS / SYDNEY / COPENHAGEN / BERLIN / MADRID / HONG KONG / TOKYO

Published by

Wise Publications
14-15 Berners Street, London W1T 3LJ, UK

Exclusive Distributors:

Music Sales Limited
Distribution Centre, Newmarket Road,
Bury St Edmunds, Suffolk IP33 3YB, UK

Music Sales Pty Limited
20 Resolution Drive,
Caringbah, NSW 2229, Australia

Order No. AM1003453
ISBN 978-1-78038-102-2
This book © Copyright 2011 Wise Publications,
a division of Music Sales Limited.

Printed in the EU

Edited by Jenni Wheeler
Backing tracks by Paul Honey

CD mixed and mastered by Jonas Persson

Your Guarantee of Quality
As publishers, we strive to produce every book
to the highest commercial standards.
The music has been freshly engraved and the book has
been carefully designed to minimise awkward page turns
and to make playing from it a real pleasure.
Particular care has been given to specifying acid-free,
neutral-sized paper made from pulps which have not been
elemental chlorine bleached. This pulp is from farmed
sustainable forests and was produced with special regard
for the environment.
Throughout, the printing and binding have been planned
to ensure a sturdy, attractive publication which should
give years of enjoyment.
If your copy fails to meet our high standards,
please inform us and we will gladly replace it.

www.musicsales.com

Hometown Glory

Words & Music by Adele Adkins

1. I've been walk-ing in the same way_____ as I_____
(2.) like it in the cit - y when_____ the air is so_____

_____ thick_____ and o - paque.
_____ did;_____

miss-ing out the cracks in the pave-
I love to see ev -'ry - bod -

- ment and tut - ting my heel_____ and strut - ting my
- y_____ in short_____ skirts, shorts_____ and shades._____

feet.
"Is there an - y - thing I can do for you,
I like it in the cit - y_____ when_____

oh,_____ the peo - ple I've__ met_____ are the

won - ders of my_____ world, are the won - ders of my_____

2° vocal ad lib.

___ world, are the won - ders of this_____ world,_____ are the

won - ders_____ of now._____

2. I ___

7

Chasing Pavements

Words & Music by Adele Adkins & Eg White

13

Make You Feel My Love

Words & Music by Bob Dylan

no doubt in my mind where you be-long.___
you ain't seen noth-ing like me yet.

3. I'd go hun-gry, I'd go black and blue,___
4. I could make you hap-py, make your dreams come true,___

I'd go crawl-ing down the av - e - nue.___ Know there's noth-ing___ that___ I___
noth-ing that I would - n't do. Go to the ends of the

would - n't do to make you feel my love.___
earth for you___ to make you feel my love,_

to make you feel my love.

Rolling In The Deep

Words & Music by Adele Adkins & Paul Epworth

Coda

Could have had it all.

Roll - ing in the deep.

You had my heart and soul 'side of your hand.

But you played it with a beat - ing.

22

Throw your soul____ through ev - 'ry o - pen door.

Drums

Count your___ bless - ings to find what you look for.

cont. sim.

Turn my___ sor - rows in - to trea - sured gold. You'll

(guitar)

Cm   N.C.

pay me___ back in kind and reap just what you've sown.____

23

Right As Rain

Words & Music by J Silverman, Adele Adkins & Leon Michels

Set Fire To The Rain

Words & Music by Fraser Smith & Adele Adkins

Someone Like You

Words & Music by Adele Adkins & Daniel Wilson

you to hold back, or hide from the light. I

hate to turn up out of the blue un-in-vit-ed but I could-n't stay a-way. I could-n't fight it. I had

hoped you'd see my face and that you'd be re-mind-ed that for me it is-n't o - ver.

1° only

2° only

38

39

Turning Tables

Words & Music by Ryan Tedder & Adele Adkins

1. Close e - nough to start a war. All that I
2. Un - der haunt - ed skies I see you. Ooh.

CD Track Listing

Full performance demonstration tracks...

1. Hometown Glory
(Adkins) Universal Music Publishing Limited

2. Chasing Pavements
(Adkins/White) Universal Music Publishing Limited

3. Make You Feel My Love
(Dylan) Sony/ATV Music Publishing (UK) Limited

4. Rolling In The Deep
(Adkins/Epworth) Universal Music Publishing Limited/EMI Music Publishing Limited

5. Right As Rain
(Silverman/Adkins/Michels)
Universal Music Publishing Limited/Kobalt Music Publishing Limited/EMI Music Limited

6. Set Fire To The Rain
(Smith/Adkins) Chrysalis Music Limited/Universal Music Publishing Limited

7. Someone Like You
(Adkins/Wilson) Universal Music Publishing Limited/Chrysalis Music Limited

8. Turning Tables
(Tedder/Adkins) Universal Music Publishing Limited/Kobalt Music Publishing Limited

Backing tracks only (without piano)...

9. Hometown Glory

10. Chasing Pavements

11. Make You Feel My Love

12. Rolling In The Deep

13. Right As Rain

14. Set Fire To The Rain

15. Someone Like You

16. Turning Tables

To remove your CD from the plastic sleeve,
lift the small lip to break the perforations.
Replace the disc after use for convenient storage.